# YOU
# ARE
# AMAZING

summersdale

YOU ARE AMAZING

An Hachette UK Company
www.hachette.co.uk

Summersdale Publishers Ltd
Part of Octopus Publishing Group Limited
Carmelite House
50 Victoria Embankment
LONDON
EC4Y 0DZ
UK

www.summersdale.com

Printed and bound in the Czech Republic

ISBN: 978-1-78685-980-8

Substantial discounts on bulk quantities of Summersdale books are available to corporations, professional associations and other organizations. For details contact general enquiries: telephone: +44 (0) 1243 771107 or email: enquiries@summersdale.com.

To..........................................

From......................................

A good head and
a good heart are
always a formidable
combination.

**Nelson Mandela**

# YOUR LIFE BELONGS TO YOU

AND YOU ALONE.

Chimamanda Ngozi Adichie

**Create the highest, grandest vision possible for your life, because you become what you believe.**

Oprah Winfrey

**Those who matter don't mind, and those who mind don't matter.**

Bernard Baruch

# You're beautiful and worthy and totally unique.

Emma Stone

Plant your garden and decorate your own soul, instead of waiting for someone to bring you flowers.

Jorge Luis Borges

**Love all, trust a few, do wrong to none.**

William Shakespeare

Life is either
a daring
adventure
or nothing.

Helen Keller

Go boldly and honestly through the world. Learn to love the fact that there is nobody else quite like you.

Daniel Radcliffe

# Our life is shaped by our mind; we become what we think.

Buddhist proverb

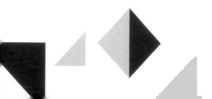

# NO MATTER WHERE YOU'RE FROM, YOUR DREAMS ARE VALID.

Lupita Nyong'o

I have insecurities, of course, but I don't hang out with anyone who points them out to me.

**Adele**

Dare to love
yourself as
if you were
a rainbow
with gold at
both ends.

Aberjhani

True happiness comes from the joy of deeds well done, the zest of creating things new.

Antoine de Saint-Exupéry

**Find something you're passionate about and keep tremendously interested in it.**

Julia Child

# You have to be odd to be number one.

Dr Seuss

# DON'T GO THROUGH LIFE; GROW THROUGH LIFE.

Eric Butterworth

# Tension is who you think you should be. Relaxation is who you are.

Chinese proverb

Do your little bit of good where you are; it's those little bits of good put together that overwhelm the world.

Desmond Tutu

# SELF-LOVE IS THE SOURCE OF ALL OUR OTHER LOVES.

Pierre Corneille

# The most powerful relationship you will ever have is the relationship with yourself.

Steve Maraboli

I avoid looking forward or backward, and try to keep looking upward.

Charlotte Brontë

You are perfectly cast in your life. I can't imagine anyone but you in the role. Go play.

**Lin-Manuel Miranda**

# NEVER DULL YOUR SHINE FOR SOMEBODY ELSE.

Tyra Banks

# What gives you pleasure and joy? Let those be the things that lead you forward in life.

Julianne Moore

# Open your heart to the sky. Live.

Adam Gnade

**Wanting to be someone else is a waste of the person you are.**

Kurt Cobain

**To free us from the expectations of others, to give us back to ourselves – there lies the great, singular power of self-respect.**

Joan Didion

# Believe you can and you're halfway there.

Theodore Roosevelt

I am not what
happened to me.
I am what I choose
to become.

Carl Jung

When I'm not feeling my best I ask myself, "What are you gonna do about it?" I use the negativity to fuel the transformation into a better me.

Beyoncé

# Do not set yourself on fire in order to keep others warm.

Anonymous

To be beautiful
means to be yourself.
You don't need to
be accepted by
others. You need to
accept yourself.

Thích Nhất Hạnh

# THE ONE THING THAT YOU HAVE THAT NOBODY ELSE HAS IS YOU.

Neil Gaiman

There's a whole category of people who miss out by not allowing themselves to be weird enough.

Alain de Botton

**The only person you are destined to become is the person you decide to be.**

Ralph Waldo Emerson

# Take the time to love yourself, and everything will be alright.

Zendaya

Whether you come
from a council
estate or a country
estate, your
success will be
determined by your
own confidence
and fortitude.

Michelle Obama

**Nourishing yourself in a way that helps you blossom in the direction you want to go is attainable, and you are worth the effort.**

Deborah Day

I am
deliberate
and afraid
of nothing.

Audre Lorde

Carve out and claim the time to care for yourself and kindle your own fire.

**Amy Ippoliti**

# There are better things ahead than any we leave behind.

C. S. Lewis

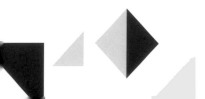

# WHATEVER YOU ARE, BE A GOOD ONE.

William Makepeace Thackeray

The reason we
struggle with
insecurity is
because we compare
our behind-
the-scenes with
everyone else's
highlight reel.

**Steve Furtick**

Success is liking yourself, liking what you do, and liking how you do it.

Maya Angelou

It's not your
job to like me –
it's mine.

Byron Katie

**Even if you fall on your face, you're still moving forward.**

Victor Kiam

# There's power in looking silly and not caring that you do.

Amy Poehler

# APPEAR AS YOU ARE, BE AS YOU APPEAR.

Rumi

I know my
strong points:
I work hard,
I have talent,
I'm funny, and
I'm a good
person.

Pink

No one will
understand you. It
is not, ultimately,
that important.
What is important
is that you
understand you.

Matt Haig

# YOUR TIME IS LIMITED, SO DON'T WASTE IT LIVING SOMEONE ELSE'S LIFE.

Steve Jobs

# In the midst of movement and chaos, keep stillness inside of you.

Deepak Chopra

You cannot protect
yourself from
sadness without
protecting yourself
from happiness.

Jonathan Safran Foer

Love yourself first and everything else falls into line. You really have to love yourself to get anything done in this world.

**Lucille Ball**

# REMIND YOURSELF THAT YOU CANNOT FAIL AT BEING YOURSELF.

Wayne W. Dyer

**If you're presenting yourself with confidence, you can pull off pretty much anything.**

Katy Perry

# Life shrinks or expands in proportion to one's courage.

Anaïs Nin

**Different is good...
So don't fit in,
don't sit still, don't
ever try to be less
than what you are.**

Angelina Jolie

You can be the ripest, juiciest peach in the world, and there's still going to be somebody who hates peaches.

Dita von Teese

**Life isn't about finding yourself. Life is about creating yourself.**

George Bernard Shaw

I may not have gone where I intended to go, but I think I have ended up where I needed to be.

Douglas Adams

Remember always that you not only have the right to be an individual, you have an obligation to be one.

Eleanor Roosevelt

You yourself, as much as anybody in the entire universe, deserve your love and affection.

Sharon Salzburg

You're always with yourself, so you might as well enjoy the company.

Diane von Fürstenberg

# TO LOVE ONESELF IS THE BEGINNING OF A LIFELONG ROMANCE.

Oscar Wilde

Never bend your head. Always hold it high. Look the world straight in the eye.

Helen Keller

# Be faithful to that which exists nowhere but within yourself.

André Gide

# Accept who you are. Unless you're a serial killer.

Ellen DeGeneres

Everyone who
got where he is
has had to begin
where he was.

Robert Louis Stevenson

# I think it is possible for ordinary people to choose to be extraordinary.

Elon Musk

Act as if what you do makes a difference. It does.

William James

You have to be
unique, and
different, and
shine in your
own way.

**Lady Gaga**

**Follow your passions, follow your heart, and the things you need will come.**

Elizabeth Taylor

# WHO WANTS TO BE NORMAL WHEN YOU CAN BE UNIQUE?

Helena Bonham Carter

I matter. I matter equally. Not "if only". Not "as long as". I matter equally. Full stop.

Chimamanda Ngozi Adichie

Don't feel stupid if you don't like what everyone else pretends to love.

There is no
reason not to be
motivated. You
cannot always be
the best. But you
can do your best.

Sebastian Vettel

**Be happy
with being you.
Love your flaws.
Own your quirks.**

Ariana Grande

The more
you give of
yourself to
life the more
life nourishes
you.

Anaïs Nin

# SET YOUR GOALS HIGH, AND DON'T STOP TILL YOU GET THERE.

Bo Jackson

**No need to hurry. No need to sparkle. No need to be anybody but oneself.**

Virginia Woolf

Focus less on the impression you're making on others and more on the impression you're making on yourself.

Amy Cuddy

# YOU ARE YOUR BEST THING.

Toni Morrison

**Always be a first-rate version of yourself, instead of a second-rate version of somebody else.**

Judy Garland

I am no bird;
and no net
ensnares me: I
am a free human
being with an
independent will.

Charlotte Brontë

The world only
exists in your
eyes… You can make
it as big or as
small as you want.

**F. Scott Fitzgerald**

# YOU ARE NEVER TOO OLD TO SET ANOTHER GOAL OR TO DREAM A NEW DREAM.

Les Brown

I don't always feel fierce and fearless, but I do feel like I'm a rock star at being human.

Tracee Ellis Ross

Your value
does not
decrease based
on someone's
inability to see
your worth.

Anonymous

We need to do a better job of putting ourselves higher on our own "to-do" list.

Michelle Obama

**Do not let what you think they think of you make you stop and question everything you are.**

Carrie Fisher

**Always be in your strength, always use your voice, and don't let anyone make you quiet.**

Amandla Stenberg

Making bad decisions doesn't make you a bad person. It is how you learn to make better choices.

Drew Barrymore

The knowledge that you have emerged wiser and stronger from setbacks means that you are, ever after, secure in your ability to survive.

J. K. Rowling

Beware; for I
am fearless. And
therefore powerful.

Mary Shelley

Don't you ever let a soul in the world tell you that you can't be exactly who you are.

**Lady Gaga**

# FOLLOW YOUR INNER MOONLIGHT; DON'T HIDE THE MADNESS.

Allen Ginsberg

**Nobody is superior, nobody is inferior, but nobody is equal either. People are simply unique, incomparable.**

Osho

# I am my own work of art.

Madonna

# Find out who you are and do it on purpose.

Dolly Parton

No matter how silly you feel or uncool you look, no matter how small that voice inside you is, that voice telling you something isn't right: listen to it.

Viv Albertine

**You don't need anybody to tell you who you are or what you are. You are what you are.**

John Lennon

The more we
do, the more
we can do.

William Hazlitt

The thing that is really hard, and really amazing, is giving up on being perfect and beginning the work of becoming yourself.

Anna Quindlen

# Keep smiling, because life is beautiful and there's so much to smile about.

Marilyn Monroe

# I'M A BIT OF A REBEL, AND I ALWAYS WILL BE.

**Neneh Cherry**

My mission in
life is not merely
to survive, but
to thrive; and
to do so with
some passion,
some compassion,
some humour and
some style.

**Maya Angelou**

Nothing is impossible, the word itself says "I'm possible"!

Audrey Hepburn

We must overcome
the notion that we
must be regular.
It robs you of
the chance to be
extraordinary.

Uta Hagen

**Sometimes the most important thing in a whole day is the rest we take between two deep breaths.**

Etty Hillesum

# Talk to yourself like you would to someone you love.

Brené Brown

# THE PRIVILEGE OF A LIFETIME IS BEING WHO YOU ARE.

Joseph Campbell

When we
give ourselves
compassion, we
are opening our
hearts in a way
that can transform
our lives.

Kristin Neff

The minute you start caring about what other people think is the minute you stop being yourself.

Meryl Streep

# A SMILE IS A CURVE THAT SETS EVERYTHING STRAIGHT.

Phyllis Diller

# If you ask me what I came to do in this world... I will answer you: I am here to live out loud!

Émile Zola

**Optimism is essential to achievement and it is also the foundation of courage.**

Nicholas Murray Butler

Your body is there
right now. You did
not have to earn a
thing. It is a gift.

**Naomi Alderman**

# WHATEVER THE MIND OF MAN CAN CONCEIVE AND BELIEVE, IT CAN ACHIEVE.

Napoleon Hill

I remind myself to be kind... to treat myself in the same gentle way I'd want to treat a daughter of mine.

Emma Stone

Live as well
as you dare.

Sydney Smith

Just throw away
all thoughts of
imaginary things,
and stand firm
in that which
you are.

Kabir

I can't change where I come from or what I've been through, so why should I be ashamed of what makes me, me?

Angie Thomas

**Become such as you are, having learned what that is.**

Pindar

All I have is all
I need and all I
need is all I have
in this moment.

Byron Katie

To accomplish
great things, we
must not only act,
but also dream;
not only plan but
also believe.

Anatole France

Whatever you did today is enough. Whatever you felt today is valid.

Brittany Burgunder

Believe in life!
Always human beings
will live and progress
to greater, broader,
and fuller life.

W. E. B. Du Bois

# IT'S NOT YOUR JOB TO BE LIKABLE. IT'S YOUR JOB TO BE YOURSELF.

Chimamanda Ngozi Adichie

You are the universe in ecstatic motion. Set your life on fire. Seek those who fan your flames.

Rumi

**Whenever you find yourself on the side of the majority, it is time to reform (or pause and reflect).**

Mark Twain

# Lighten up on yourself. No one is perfect. Gently accept your humanness.

Deborah Day

I am glad that
I paid so little
attention to good
advice; had I abided
by it I might have
been saved from
some of my most
valuable mistakes.

Edna St Vincent Millay

# THIS ABOVE ALL: TO THINE OWN SELF BE TRUE.

William Shakespeare

May you live every day of your life.

Jonathan Swift

When we can see ourselves as we truly are and accept ourselves, we build the necessary foundation for self-love.

bell hooks

**Invent your world.
Surround yourself
with people, colour,
sounds, and work
that nourish you.**

Susan Ariel Rainbow Kennedy

IT TAKES
COURAGE TO
GROW UP
AND BECOME
WHO YOU
REALLY ARE.

E. E. Cummings

Dig within.
There lies the
well-spring of
good: ever dig, and
it will ever flow.

**Marcus Aurelius**

We are all creatures of the stars.

Doris Lessing

The most creative act you will ever undertake is the act of creating yourself.

Deepak Chopra

# One of the secrets of a happy life is continuous small treats.

Iris Murdoch

# Just be yourself – there is no one better.

Taylor Swift

# WHO LOOKS OUTSIDE, DREAMS. WHO LOOKS INSIDE, AWAKES.

Carl Jung

**To be yourself in a world that is constantly trying to make you something else is the greatest accomplishment.**

Ralph Waldo Emerson

If you hear a voice within you say "You are not a painter", then by all means paint... and that voice will be silenced.

Vincent van Gogh

# BE IN LOVE WITH YOUR LIFE, EVERY DETAIL OF IT.

Jack Kerouac

# I exist as I am, that is enough.

Walt Whitman

If we all did the
things we are
capable of doing,
we would literally
astound ourselves.

Thomas Edison

You're only here for a short visit. Don't hurry, don't worry, and be sure to smell the flowers along the way.

**Walter Hagen**

# CHOOSE PEOPLE WHO LIFT YOU UP.

Michelle Obama

I promise you
that each and
every one of you
is made to be
who you are.

Selena Gomez

# There is just one life for each of us: our own.

**Euripides**

**The key to happiness is being happy by yourself and for yourself.**

Ellen DeGeneres

We have to dare
to be ourselves,
however
frightening
or strange that
self might
prove to be.

May Sarton

If you're interested in finding out more about our books, find us on Facebook at Summersdale Publishers and follow us on Twitter at @Summersdale.

www.summersdale.com